CURRENT QUOTES:

Intriguing Insights from Today's Top Icons, Influencers and Innovators

Compiled by Sam Horn,
Founder of The Intrigue Institute

"It's not melodramatic to say there are times when your destiny hangs on the impression you make."

-BARBARA WALTERS

WESTCOM PRESS

New York   Los Angeles   Washington DC

Westcom Press
2101 N Street, NW
Suite T-1
Washington, DC 20037

westcomassociates@mac.com

18 17 16 15 14 13 12 11 1 2 3 4 5

ISBN: 978-0-9835003-5-3

Library of Congress Number: 2011940016

Introduction

I see the world through quote-colored glasses. When did it all start?

On a rainy Thanksgiving day in Southern California.

I was 10 and we were visiting our grandparents in Los Angeles.

Instead of the typical California sunshine, it was cold, gray.

My brother, sister and cousins and I couldn't play outside so we were banished to Granny's screened-in porch and told, "Occupy yourself" until turkey would be served at 4 pm.

What to do?

Well, I was an inveterate reader.

Growing up in a small town, the library was often the most exciting thing going on.

So, as soon as I spied a stack of *Reader's Digests*, I knew how I was spending my afternoon. I eagerly tackled them and emerged, hours later, with little torn-out pieces of paper with quotes and jokes.

That was my first introduction to the power of crafted language – a powerfully turned phrase or one-liner – to entertain, educate, enlighten and move "beyond words."

I've been tearing out "little pieces of paper" ever since from newspapers and magazines.

Every time I see something that touches my heart, gets my eyebrows up or makes me laugh, I tear it out and share it with my audiences or readers. (I'm an author/motivational speaker who's had the privilege of speaking to groups around the world – from Boston to Berlin, Denver to Dublin.)

I also post quotes on my refrigerator to keep them "in sight, in mind."

They help me be a better person.

They remind me of how I want to see the world – with gratitude and appreciation.

They help me laugh – even when things aren't particularly funny at that moment.

They cause me to stop, wonder and rethink what I thought I knew to be true.

I hope these quotes do the same for you.

I've spent a lot of time collecting and curating them.

What's different about them? *You have to be alive to be included.*

Why is that important?

Well, as The Intrigue Expert, I have studied the art and science of "intrigue" for 20+ years.

Intrigue is "the ability to pique curiosity, to capture interest."

One of the most important things I've learned is that people are BBB -- Busy. Bored. Been-there-heard-that. They make up their mind *in the first 60 seconds* whether we're worth their valuable time and mind.

For something to capture our attention; it needs to be startlingly relevant and/or something we haven't heard before.

Classic quotes (which often come across as clichés) don't have the power do that.

As soon as we roll out a familiar saying from Socrates, Churchill or Lao Tzu, people roll their eyes and tune out.

It's not that profound quotes from Eleanor Roosevelt, JFK, MLK and Ralph Waldo Emerson aren't *true* – they're just not *new*.

So, what can we do?

We can introduce intriguing content and current quotes from today's icons that get people's eyebrows up.

What do I mean by "get people's eyebrows up?"

Try it right now. Arch your eyebrows.

Do you feel curious? Like you want to know more?

That means what you heard or saw just got in your mental door.

It means instead of this information being boring or obvious, it's *intriguing*.

Being interesting is what we crave as individuals and that's our goal as communicators.

This book is a treasure trove of intriguing insights that have the power to make your day.

You are invited to use this book as a perpetual calendar.

Reading the right words, at the right time, is a wonderful way to start the day.

Some of the quotes are profound, some inspiring, some provocative, some funny. All have the power to act as a mood vitamin.

You may be tempted to read this book all at once. You might want to use the index to find a quote on a particular topic or by a favorite author.

Go ahead.

But then go back. Keep this book by your kitchen table, desk or nightstand.

Take one minute to read and savor that day's quote as part of your morning ritual.

You wouldn't gulp down a fine wine . . . don't gulp down fine wisdom.

Take a moment . . .just a moment to . . .

- Ponder.
- Reflect.
- Absorb.
- Adopt, adapt and integrate.
- Act.

Ask yourself:

"How is this quote relevant for me?"

"How can it help me be a better person?"

"How can it help me remember to be more grateful, more giving, more gracious?"

"How can it help me lighten up and keep a sense of humor about myself and my circumstances?"

"How can it help me adopt a more positive, pro-active approach to life?"

At the end of this book, you'll discover a bonus section on how to "hook and hinge" these current quotes into your written and spoken communication so it POP!s.

For now, simply turn the page and . . . read 'em and reap . . . and attribute!

"We've got to follow
through on our ideals
or we betray something
at the heart of
who we are."

— BONO

"If you listen to your
heart, you'll remember
who you were all along."

— MAKANA

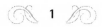

"Life is a series of commas, not periods."

- MATTHEW MCCONAUGHEY

"There are no regrets in life, just lessons."

- JENNIFER ANNISTON

"Sing with passion.
Work with laughter.
Love with heart.
'Cause that's all that
matters in the end."

- KRIS KRISTOFFERSON

"When you lose, you're
more motivated. When
you win, you fail to
see your mistakes and
probably no one can tell
you anything."

- VENUS WILLIAMS

7

"I learned how to win by losing and not liking it."

- TOM WATSON

8

"The need for change bulldozed a road down the center of my mind."

- MAYA ANGELOU

9

"You must consider the bottom line, but make it integrity before profits."

- DENIS WAITLEY

10

"I have heard every excuse on the planet – except for a good one."

- BOB GREENE

11

"Being rich isn't about
having a lot of money;
it's about having
a lot of options."

\- Chris Rock

12

"I don't want life to
imitate art.
I want life to be art."

\- Carrie Fisher

"It is our choices that
show us who we
truly are,
far more than our
abilities."

- J.K. ROWLING

"The very least you can
do in your life is to figure
out what you hope for. . .
and then live
inside that hope."

- BARBARA KINGSOLVER

"Being happy is something you have to learn. I often surprise myself by saying 'Wow, this is it. I guess I'm happy. I got a home I love. A career I love. I'm even feeling more at peace with myself. If there's something else to happiness, let me know."

- HARRISON FORD

"I don't believe in guilt, I believe in living on impulse as long as you never intentionally hurt another person, and don't judge people in your life. I think you should live completely free."

- ANGELINA JOLIE

17

"If you smile when no one else is around, you really mean it."

- ANDY ROONEY

18

"Pain is temporary. Quitting is forever."

– LANCE ARMSTRONG

19

"I can get sad, I can get frustrated, I can get scared, but I never get depressed - because there's joy in my life."

- MICHAEL J. FOX

20

"Live out of your imagination, not your history."

- STEPHEN COVEY

"Are you doing what you're doing today because you want to do it, or because it's what you were doing yesterday?"

- DR. PHIL MCGRAW

"We are not held back by the love we didn't receive in the past, but by the love we're not extending in the present."

- MARIANNE WILLIAMSON

23

"People treat you the way
you teach them
to treat you."

- JACK CANFIELD

24

"To me, if life boils
down to one thing,
it's movement.
To live is to
keep moving."

- JERRY SEINFELD

25

"Creativity is allowing yourself to make mistakes. Art is knowing which ones to keep."

- SCOTT ADAMS

26

"Art is the only way to run away without leaving home."

- TWYLA THARP

27

"The greatest thing
you can do
is surprise yourself."

- STEVE MARTIN

28

"Good teams become
great ones when the
members trust each
other enough to
surrender the 'me'
for the 'we.'"

- PHIL JACKSON

29

"No one wants to go out mid-sentence."

- JOHNNY DEPP

30

"Life is 50% what you make it and 50% how you take it."

– OPRAH WINFREY

"If you are not being bullied, be someone that nurtures. If there's someone in your class that maybe doesn't have a lot of friends, be the person that sits with them in the cafeteria sometimes. Be the bigger person."

- LADY GAGA

"Have I pushed the
envelope as much as I
want to? Not yet.
That's why I'm still
creatively hungry."

- Steven Spielberg

"Integrity
is so perishable
in the
summer months
of success."

- Vanessa Redgrave

"The role of the musician is to go from concept to full execution. Put another way, it's to go from understanding the content of something to really learning how to communicate it and make sure it's well-received and lives in somebody else."

- Yo-Yo Ma

"I finally figured out the only reason to be alive is to enjoy it."

- RITA MAE BROWN

"In my last year of school, I was voted Class Optimist and Class Pessimist. Looking back, I realize they were only half right."

- JACK NICHOLSON

"I wish there were ten of me and we could each be doing what we wanted."

- GEORGE LUCAS

"Do something you really love that you would do anyway and if there's a genuine need for it and it helps other people, you're home."

- DIANE SAWYER

21

"What's dangerous is not to evolve."

- JEFF BEZOS

"There's no such thing as a wrong note as long as you're singing."

- PETE SEEGER

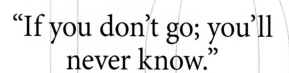

"If you don't go; you'll never know."

- ROBERT DE NIRO

"Persistence isn't using the same tactics over and over. That's just annoying. Persistence is having the same goal over and over."

- SETH GODIN

"There's a great freedom
when you have your feet
in two so called mutually
exclusive worlds:
The world of irony, and
the world of soul,
The world of flesh, and
the world of spirit,
The world of surface and
the world of depth."

- BONO

"I really don't want to wax philosophic, but if you're alive, you've got to flap your arms and legs and make a lot of noise, because life is the very opposite of death. And therefore, as I see it, if you're quiet, you're not living. You've got to be noisy, or at least your thoughts should be noisy and colorful and lively."

- MEL BROOKS

14

"Talent is a flame.
Genius is a fire."

- BERN WILLIAMS

15

"You can't wring your
hands and roll up your
sleeves at the same time."

- PAT SCHROEDER

"I've yet to be on a campus where most women weren't worrying about some aspect of combining marriage, children, and a career. I've yet to find one where many men were worrying about the same thing."

- GLORIA STEINEM

"Keep in mind that you're more interested in what you have to say than anyone else is."

- ANDY ROONEY

"You know, we don't grow most of the food we eat. We wear clothes other people make. We speak a language that other people developed. We use a mathematics that other people evolved... I mean, we're constantly taking things. It's a wonderful, ecstatic feeling to create something that puts it back in the pool of human experience and knowledge."

- STEVE JOBS

"If you only believe that you're an artist when you have a big advance in your pocket and a single coming out, I would say that's quite soulless. You have to have a sense of your own greatness and your own ability from a deep place inside you. I am the one with the litmus test in my hands of what people need to hear next."

- LADY GAGA

"Love is what we were born with. Fear is what we learned here."

- MARIANNE WILLIAMSON

"It takes 20 years to build a reputation and five minutes to ruin it. If you think about that, you'll do things differently."

- WARREN BUFFETT

"Women are the most powerful magnet in the universe. All men are cheap metal and we know where North is."

— LARRY MILLER

"Secret: It's not the writing part that's hard. What's hard is sitting down to write."

- STEVEN PRESSFIELD

24

"Don't be yourself – be someone a little nicer."

- MIGNON McLAUGHLIN

25

"Anything in life that we don't accept will make trouble for us until we make peace with it."

- SHAKTI GAWAIN

"Business is difficult. But it could be approached two ways: Seriously, or with an entertainment aspect, with pleasure, with fun. And we decided to try to make our work as fun as our creativity."

- GUY LALIBERTE'

"Enough about me. What do you think about me?"

- BETTE MIDLER'S CHARACTER IN THE MOVIE *Beaches*

"If we learn to open our hearts, anyone, including the people who drive us crazy, can be our teacher."

- PEMA CHODRON

"You don't get harmony when everybody sings the same note."

- DOUG FLOYD

"I've been doing a lot of
abstract painting lately,
extremely abstract. No
brush, no paint, no
canvas. I just think
about it."

- STEPHEN WRIGHT

"The way I see it, if you
want the rainbow, you
gotta put up with the
rain."

- DOLLY PARTON

"If you don't overlook
the fact of what you look
like, no one else will. I
used to get booed off
the stage and I thought
it was because I was
white. There comes a
time when you gotta stop
thinking like that and
just be you."

- EMINEM

"True wealth is discretionary time."

- ALAN WEISS

"I think of life as a good book. The further you get into it; the more it comes together and makes sense."

- RABBI HAROLD KUSHNER

When asked why he chose not to stage a summer concert tour for the first time in 17 years, country singer Kenny Chesney said, "My career is great. I don't need more money or fame. I need more heart."

7

"You miss 100% of the shots you never take."

– WAYNE GRETZKY

8

"When I die, I want to come back as me."

- MARK CUBAN

"The secret is to enjoy
being you."

- Diane von Furstenberg

"Men are allowed
to have passion and
commitment for their
work... a woman is
allowed that feeling for a
man, but not her work."

- Barbra Streisand

11

"When I swim, I don't feel old, I feel eternal."

- DIANA NYAD

12

"Are you frittering away your greatness?"

- KEITH YAMASHITA

"For to be free is not merely to cast off one's chains, but to live in a way that respects and enhances the freedom of others."

- NELSON MANDELA

On *CBS Sunday Morning*, Robin Williams was asked what he's learned about life at age sixty, "You've got the gig. There's no rush. Just enjoy it."

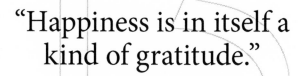

"Happiness is in itself a
kind of gratitude."

- Joseph Wood Krutch

"If I'd had some set idea
of a finish line, don't
you think I would have
crossed it years ago?"

- Bill Gates

17

"I always love it when you feel like all bets are off. I'm a fan of never feeling safe."

- DREW BARRYMORE

18

"Love elevates. Love is what you live for."

- ANGELINA JOLIE

"We have had challenging times, but there was not one single moment when I thought we couldn't overcome the challenges."

– HOWARD SCHULTZ

"Dreaming, after all, is a form of planning."

– GLORIA STEINEM

21

"Writers get to live life twice."

- ANNE LAMOTT

22

"The man who has no imagination has no wings."

- MUHAMMAD ALI

23

"Whenever I'm under pressure, I remember to have fun."

- JEFF BRIDGES

24

"I want compassion to be the new black."

– STEPHEN TYLER

"Labels are for filing.
Labels are for clothing.
Labels are not for
people."

- MARTINA NAVRATILOVA

"Anything you're rigid
about, sooner or later, the
rug is going to get pulled
out from under you."

- ALAN ARKIN

"Not what we *have* but what we *enjoy* constitutes our abundance."

- JOHN PETIT-SENN

"What's next? I don't really plan it. You just hope a swell shows up and you're ready."

- BETHANY HAMILTON (AKA SOUL SURFER)

"It is not uncommon for people to spend their whole life waiting to start living."

- ECKHART TOLLE

"There's a lot more power in calm than in vituperation."

- DENNIS PRAGER

31

"If they give you ruled paper, write the other way."

- JUAN RAMON JIMENEZ

"Fear is a pair of handcuffs on your soul."

- FAYE DUNAWAY

"I've never understood the concept of having something to fall back on. If I'm going to fall, I want to fall ... forward. And if I get knocked down, I get back up."

- DENZEL WASHINGTON

"Many people are
searching for happiness
like it's out there
somewhere. It's not. It's
in *here*. It's in our ability
to look around,
at any given moment,
and celebrate what's
right with our world,
right now."

- SAM HORN

"The truth of the matter
is that you always know
the right thing to do. The
hard part is doing it."

— Norman Schwarzkopf

"There is a fountain
of youth: It is in your
mind, your talents,
creativity and the lives
of the people you love.
When you tap this
source, you defeat age."

— Sophia Loren

"I was terrified of flying. My dad told me, 'Think of turbulence as rough waves that hit a boat. It might get choppy, but you know you won't sink.'"

– LUKE RUSSERT

"If you just set out to be liked you would be prepared to compromise on anything at any time and you would achieve nothing."

– MARGARET THATCHER

"Remember that sometimes not getting what you want is a wonderful stroke of luck."

- DALAI LAMA

"When you lose, you have to figure out what you did, what you didn't do and what you want to do next time you're in that situation . . . and then go do it."

- JACK NICKLAUS

10

"I can't wait to get out there and sing every night. I just love it. There's still a magic spark. When that's gone; I'll stop."

- ROD STEWART

11

"Everyone has a 'What I Really Want to Do' career."

- LANARKA ROSE

12

"Discipline is
remembering
what you want."

- DAVID CAMPBELL

13

"One person's craziness is
another person's reality."

- TIM BURTON

"I'm finally enjoying the
taste of healthy food.
I feel better than I have
in years. It's like I'm
aging backward."

- DONNA BRAZILE

"If you listen to your
fears, you will die never
knowing what a great
person you might
have been."

- ROBERT H. SCHULLER

"If you're not willing to lose, then you'll do whatever it takes to win; and you become someone you're not."

- KATIE COURIC

"I started out wanting to write great poems, then wanting to discover true poems. Now, I want to be the poem."

- MARK NEPO

18

"As long as I'm in good shape, you'll always see me smiling."

- USAIN BOLT

19

"You can do anything, but not everything."

– DAVID ALLEN

"During those times you feel stuck or even that you're slipping backward, you may actually be backing up to get a running start."

- DAN MILLMAN

"I've never worked a day in my life because I love what I do and I still have a lot to learn."

- TONY BENNETT

"Resentment isn't a magnetic personal style."

- Peggy Noonan

"To be successful, we must live from our imaginations, not from our memories."

- Steven Covey

24

"I like marriage.
The idea."

– Toni Morrison

25

"I've always had a
sense of being alone,
a solitary man. That's
why I like Twitter. It's
instant gratification. I
get responses almost
immediately from
everywhere in the world."

– Neil Diamond

26

"When you learn, teach.
When you get, give."

-MAYA ANGELOU

27

"Don't ever wrestle with
a pig. You'll both get
dirty but the pig
will enjoy it."

– CALE YARBOROUGH

"Young people in the business have grown up and made the wrong decisions, or bad decisions, and haven't been good role models. To be someone people look up to is important to me."

- JUSTIN BIEBER

"When was the last time you looked at the stars with the wonder they deserved?"

- KRIS KRISTOFFERSON

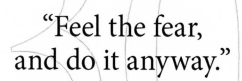

"Feel the fear,
and do it anyway."

- SUSAN JEFFERS

"I rant, therefore I am."

- Dennis Miller

"Entrepreneurs who
focus on ONE thing,
will always do better
than those who
try to do everything."

- Mark Zuckerberg

"I wanted to be a forest
ranger. At a very early
age, I knew I didn't want
to do what my dad did,
which was work
in an office."

- HARRISON FORD

"I have become my own
version of an optimist.
If I can't make it through
one door, I'll go
through another – or
I'll make a door."

- JOAN RIVERS

"I would like to do more dramas when I find a good role that will allow me to politely upset people's expectations of me as a comic actor."

- BEN STILLER

"The best compliment you can be given is when your kids want to come home and spend time with you. I'm radically grateful."

- SUSAN SARANDON

7

"There cannot be a crisis next week. My schedule is already full."

- HENRY KISSINGER

8

"How people treat you is their karma; how you react is yours."

- WAYNE DYER

"My religion is very simple. My religion is kindness."

- Dalai Llama

"The bear is what we all wrestle with. Everybody has their bear in life. It's about conquering that bear and letting him go…"

- Jennifer Lopez

11

"You never really lose until you stop trying."

- MIKE DITKA

12

"It took me a long time to not judge myself through someone else's eyes."

- SALLY FIELD

"Losing everything you thought you wanted can be the first step to finding what you need."

- Katie Lee

"It's never too late, in fiction or in life, to revise."

- Nancy Thayer

"You've got to give
yourself a little time to
live a lot of things
so you can write about
a lot of things."

- TAYLOR SWIFT (EXPLAINING THE 2-YEAR
"GAP" BETWEEN HER ALBUMS)

"I need people who know
me, and also people
who don't know me and
who push me to think
differently and be the
best me I can be."

- MICHELLE OBAMA

"If you had to identify, in one word, the reason why the human race has not achieved, and never will achieve, its full potential, that word would be . . . meetings."

- DAVE BARRY

"Cherish forever what makes you unique, 'cuz you're really a yawn if it goes."

- BETTE MIDLER

19

"Life is not fair;
get used to it."

- BILL GATES

20

"I work from the gut.
You can tell any story
20 different ways. The
trick is to pick one
and go with it."

- CLINT EASTWOOD ON WHY HE SHOOTS ONE
OR TWO TAKES OF A MOVIE SCENE
INSTEAD OF THE NORMAL 12-20 TIMES
MOST DIRECTORS DO.

"Your present circumstances don't determine where you can go; they merely determine where you start."

- NIDO QUBEIN

"Numb is the new deep, done with the old me, and talk is the same cheap it's been."

- JOHN MAYER

23

"Here's my motto - if you're not happy at home, you're not happy anywhere else."

- ANGIE HARMON

24

"I didn't want to be a good wife; I wanted to be a hot date."

- DIANE KEATON ON WHY SHE'S NEVER MARRIED

25

"Insomnia is my greatest inspiration."

- JON STEWART

26

"I've been long overdue for a date with happiness."

- MATTHEW RUTLIN

"Discipline is the refining fire by which talent becomes ability."

- ROY L. SMITH

"If you're going to be able to look back on something and laugh about it, you might as well laugh about it now."

- MARIE OSMOND

A reporter asked Brigadier
General Wilma Vaught,
"What did
you want to be when
you grew up?"
Her quick response was,
"In charge!"

"Don't say you don't have
enough time. You have
exactly the same number
of hours per day that were
given to Helen Keller,
Michelangelo, Mother
Teresa, Leonardo da Vinci
and Albert Einstein."

- H. JACKSON BROWN

"I like being tested. I get as scared as anyone. But the feeling of putting yourself on the line, putting your talent out there, betting on yourself and having it work, is the most exhilarating feeling in the world."

- CONAN O'BRIEN

"It has always surprised me how little attention philosophers have paid to humor since it is a more significant process of mind than reason. Reasons can only sort out perceptions; humor is involved in changing them."

- EDWARD DE BONO

"When I saw Ellen DeGeneres at the cover shoot for O, I didn't even have to ask how she was; it showed on her face. It radiated the type of happiness and peace that only happens when we're living at our highest potential."

- OPRAH WINFREY

"I don't believe in pitfalls. I believe in not doing the same thing twice."

- GUY LALIBERTE'

"I can't give you the formula for success. I can for failure. Try to please everyone."

- BILL COSBY

Reporters kept asking
San Francisco 49er Jerry
Rice if he was the top
receiver in the NFL.
He finally said, "I feel
like I'm the best; but
you're not going to get
me to say that."

"The minute you settle
for less than you deserve,
you get even less than
you settled for."

- MAUREEN DOWD

"Fear saps passion. Don't cheat the world of your contribution. Give it what you've got."

- STEVEN PRESSFIELD

"We'll love you just the way you are if you're perfect."

- ALANIS MORISSETTE

"Hunches and
coincidences are your
SerenDestiny® calling."

- SAM HORN

"Argue for your
limitations, and sure
enough, they're yours."

- RICHARD BACH

"What is exciting is not for one person to be stronger than the other…but for two people to have met their match and yet they are equally as stubborn, as obstinate, as passionate, as crazy as the other."

– Barbra Streisand

"The future is completely open, and we are writing it moment to moment."

- Pema Chodron

13

"How do you know what's right in front of you when you're looking the other way?"

- ANNA QUINDLEN

14

"We pretend it's hard to follow our heart's dreams. Truth is, it's difficult to avoid walking through the many doors that open."

- JULIA CAMERON

"I'm on the patch right now. Where it releases small dosages of approval until I no longer crave it, and then I'm gonna rip it off."

- ELLEN DEGENERES

"My happiness grows in direct proportion to my acceptance and in inverse proportion to my expectations."

- MICHAEL J. FOX

17

"People say I'm indecisive; but I don't know about that."

- GEORGE BUSH

18

"No one has wasted time the way I have. It was 1979, I looked up, it was 2007."

- FRAN LEBOWITZ

"Ask people, 'What is your passion?' and they often freeze. They feel they have to give an amazing answer like, 'feeding the orphans of the world.' Or they feel as if, 'I don't know', isn't an option."

- DAN PINK

In a *Washington Post* interview with Michael Phelps about why he had decided to rededicate himself to swimming after 4 months of partying following the Olympics. He replied, "Having nothing but fun is not all that fun."

"I don't think of myself as a brand. What I think about is, 'How do I get better? How do I make the kind of movies I want to see and hope others do too.'"

- J.J. ABRAMS

"A leader is one who knows the way, goes the way, and shows the way."

- JOHN C. MAXWELL

23

"The only thing worse than being alone is wishing you were."

\- CAROLYN HAX

24

"What if I don't want to be just okay. What if I want to be extraordinary?"

\- WILL SMITH

"One of the very first
things I figured out
about life…is that it's
better to be a grateful
person than a grumpy
one, because you have to
live in the same
world either way,
and if you're hopeful,
you have more fun."

- BARBARA KINGSOLVER

"Where do you go to
replenish yourself?
This is not a luxury,
it's a necessity if
we don't want our
energy to run dry.
Each of us needs a free
place, a little psychic
territory. Do you have
yours?"

- GLORIA STEINEM

27

"Dream . . . it gives the heavens something to work with."

- TRISH WHYNOT

28

"Action is the antidote to despair."

- JOAN BAEZ

"Before I met my
husband, I'd never fallen
in love. I'd stepped
in it a few times."

– RITA RUDNER

"Mentally, the only
players who survive in
the pros are the ones
able to manage all their
responsibilities."

- TOM BRADY

"Charisma is not character."

- LAURA LINNEY

"My experience has been that the people who talk the loudest about morality are the people who possess the least amount of it."

- JAMES CARVILLE

"I've finally realized if it's not happening now; it's not happening. No reason to pre-freak out about problems."

- AIMEE MANN

"Jerry Maguire was just a movie. No one completes you."

- OPRAH WINFREY

"I've never really been
anywhere, and now
I get to go everywhere.
I just have to make sure
there's enough memory
on my computer to hold
all my pictures."

- CARRIE UNDERWOOD

"As a parent, I've learned
kids spell love…t-i-m-e.
You can never give your
kids enough time."

- KYLE CHANDLER

"I want to write songs that play themselves - songs that sweep you up in their current."

– K.D. Lang

"A lot of the time, I'm raising more questions than I'm answering."

- Andy Carvin

"As long as you're going to think, you might as well think big!"

- DONALD TRUMP

"I would look at a dog and when our eyes met, I realized that the dog and all creatures are my family. They're like you and me."

—ZIGGY MARLEY

"We need to treat each other with consideration. In my world, the squeaky wheel does not get the grease."

- TIM GUNN

"My winning is getting to perform. That's my victory."

- KELLY CLARKSON

13

"Women like myself,
CEOs, can pave the
way for more women
to get to the top."

– ANDREA JUNG

14

"I would rather have a
mind opened by wonder
than one closed
by belief."

- GERRY SPENCE

"People only notice stuff that is new and different. You have to tell a story, not give a lecture. You have to hint at the facts, not announce them… because the process of discovery is far more powerful than being told the right answer."

- SETH GODIN

"I've always thought
with relationships, that
it's more about what you
bring to the table than
what you're going to get
from it. It's very nice if
you sit down and the
cake appears. But if
you go to the table
expecting cake, then
it's not so good."

– ANJELICA HUSTON

17

"I am the world's oldest teenager. I've never lost my youthful attitude."

— RODNEY DANGERFIELD

18

"I gravitate towards gravitas."

— MORGAN FREEMAN

When *The Power of One* author Bryce Courtenay was asked at the Maui Writers Conference what the secret was to finishing a book, he growled, "Bum glue!"

"If you wait to write, you're not a writer, you're a waiter."

- DAN POYNTER

"We went through a tough time and made it out the other side. I kept telling my team, 'The only way we can screw this up is by not being bold enough.'"

- CONAN O'BRIEN

"Stop looking at me in that tone of voice."

– DANE COOK

"It's only words . . .
unless they're true."

- DAVID MAMET

"I'm a human being
and I fall in love
and sometimes I
don't have control of
every situation."

- BEYONCÉ KNOWLES

25

"Anybody who worries
all day is going to fret
their life away."

- KATIE COURIC

26

"We can't plan life.
All we can do is be
available for it."

- LAURYN HILL

"I have forced myself to begin writing when I've been utterly exhausted, when I've felt my soul as thin as a playing card and somehow the activity of writing changes everything."

- JOYCE CAROL OATES

"The purpose of life is a life of purpose."

- ROBERT BYRNE

"If you talk to a man
in a language he
understands, that goes
to his head. If you talk to
him in his language, that
goes to his heart."

– NELSON MANDELA

"It's better to hang out
with people better than
you. Pick out associates
whose behavior is better
than yours and you'll
drift in that direction."

- WARREN BUFFETT

"When it happens, I want to stop the match and shout, 'That's what it's all about!' Because it is. It's not the big prize I'm going to win at the end of the match. It's having done something totally pure, having experienced the perfect emotion."

- BILLIE JEAN KING

"I'm always happy.
Sometimes I just forget."

- JENNIFER EGAN

"Talent wins games,
but teamwork and
intelligence wins
championships."

- MICHAEL JORDAN

"Did you ever wonder
why no one ever
tries softer?"

- LILLY TOMLIN

"I love leading a quiet
life and then having little
binges of seeing people.
I love them both. I don't
want to have either of
them all the time."

- W.S. MERWIN

"I don't like guys who
will lie down and take it.
I want someone who'll
fight back. I like people
who can argue well."

– SANDRA BULLOCK

"Women need real
moments of solitude
and self-reflection to
balance out how much of
ourselves we give away."

- BARBARA DE ANGELIS

"Twitter is compatible with the way I think as a songwriter. There's a limit to the number of characters you can use, and when you write a song you have to tell your story in 100-150 words. It's natural for me."

– NEIL DIAMOND

"At the end of the day, looking back at your life, you want to have minimized the number of regrets you have. That's what should drive us – not how much money we have. It's regrets that will haunt us in the end."

– Jeff Bezos

"Our soul-mate is the person who makes life come to life."

- RICHARD BACH

"When asked if she'd stop to tread water on her swim from Cuba to Key West, 61 year old Diana Nyad said, "Why would I rest? It means I'm not going anywhere."

"Everybody has a calling.
Your real job in life is to
figure out what that is,
embrace it and use it
to serve the world."

OPRAH, FROM HER LAST SHOW
(SAM HORN CALLS THAT SERENDESTINY®)

"To have what you've
never had, you must be
willing to do what you've
never done. My motto is,
'Resist nothing.'"

- SERENDESTINEER MARY LOVERDE

125

13

"The best way to make your dreams come true is to wake up."

- MUHAMMAD ALI

14

"I have found there is no substitute for paying attention."

- DIANE SAWYER

On the TV show *Friends*, Phoebe was complaining about something her brother did. Joey got exasperated and finally said, "Phoebe, have you told him how you feel?" "Yes. Well . . . not out loud."

"Clarity affords focus."

- Thomas Leonard

"We need a
12-step group
for non-stop talkers.
We're going to call it,
On and On Anon."

- PAULA POUNDSTONE

"I skate to where the
puck is going to be, not
where it has been."

– WAYNE GRETZKY

19

"Books in your head help no one."

- SAM HORN

20

"My challenge now is finding the optimum (not the minimum or the maximum) level of training."

- MICHAEL PHELPS

"Taking a risk is part
of my DNA.
You cannot achieve
great things if you don't
take great risks."

- GUY LALIBERTE'

"Needless to say, we
didn't have Facebook
growing up . . .
we had a phonebook."

- BETTY WHITE

"If you can't get along with people, you don't belong in this business; because that's all we have around here."

- Lee Iacocca

"That's the sign of a good life decision, when you don't waver from it or second-guess it."

- Steve Carell (on why he knew it was time to leave the TV show The Office)

25

"For most people, the opposite of talking is not listening; it's waiting."

- FRAN LIEBOWITZ

26

"I was a Brownie for a day. My mom made me stop. She didn't want me to conform."

– SANDRA BULLOCK

27

"No, please tell me again about the problem you won't take any steps to solve."

- CAROLYN HAX

28

"Guard your good mood."

- MERYL STREEP

"The internet is just a world passing around notes in a classroom."

- JON STEWART

"The trouble with the rat race is that even if you win, you're still a rat."

- LILLY TOMLIN

"Be a yardstick of quality. Some people aren't used to an environment where excellence is expected."

- STEVE JOBS

"All adventures into new territory are scary."

- SALLY RIDE

"When one's expectations are reduced to zero, one really appreciates everything one does have."

- STEPHEN HAWKING

"Mistakes are part
of the dues one pays
for a full life."

- SOPHIA LOREN

"History passes the
final judgment."

- SIDNEY POITIER

"Go slowly, breathe
and smile."

– THICH NHAT HANH

"The cow runs away from
the storm while the buffalo
charges toward it—and
gets through it faster.
When I'm confronted with
a tough challenge, I do
not prolong the torment. I
become the buffalo."

- DONNA BRAZILE

"Everyone is entitled to
my opinion."

- MADONNA

"Try to open a path
through that maze,
put a little order in
that chaos."

- ISABEL ALLENDE

"When you create, you get a little endorphin rush. Why do you think Einstein looked like that?"

- ROBIN WILLIAMS

"I try to believe like I believed when I was five... when your heart tells you everything you need to know."

- LUCY LIU

11

"Only dead fish swim with the stream all the time."

- LINDA ELLERBEE

12

"This is what I want in heaven... words to become notes and conversations to be symphonies."

– TINA TURNER

13

"The world is not made up of atoms, it's made up of stories."

- MURIEL RUKEYSER

14

"The more specific you are; the more universal you are."

- NANCY HALE

"I cried over beauty, I cried over pain, and the other time I cried because I felt nothing. I can't help it. I'm just a cliché of myself."

- KEANU REEVES

"It is impossible to live without failing at something, unless you live so cautiously that you might as well not have lived at all - in which case, you fail by default."

- J.K. ROWLING

"People are like stained-glass windows. They sparkle and shine when the sun is out, but when the darkness sets in, their true beauty is revealed only if there is light from within."

- ELISABETH KÜBLER-ROSS

"Chase your passion, not your pension."

– DENIS WAITLEY

"At a certain point,
I just felt, you know,
God is not looking for
alms, God is looking
for action. We've got
to follow through on
our ideals or we betray
something at the heart
of who we are."

- BONO

"So what do we do?
Anything. Something.
So long as we just don't
sit there. If we mess it up,
start over. Try something
else. If we wait until
we've satisfied all the
uncertainties, it may
be too late."

- LEE IACOCCA

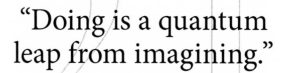

"Doing is a quantum
leap from imagining."

- BARBARA SHER

"Good enough never is."

- DEBBI FIELDS

23

"Creativity is like looking through a kaleidoscope. You look at a set of elements, the same ones everyone else see, but then reassemble those floating bits and pieces into an enticing new possibility."

- ROSABETH MOSS KANTER

24

"I am two with nature."

- WOODY ALLEN

"I've worked too hard and too long to let anything stand in the way of my goals. I will not let my teammates down and I will not let myself down."

- MIA HAMM

"Nature is so powerful, so strong. Capturing its essence is not easy - your work becomes a dance with light and the weather. It takes you to a place within yourself."

– ANNIE LEIBOWITZ

27

"If you've got a talent, protect it."

- JIM CARREY

28

"One way to keep momentum going is to have constantly greater goals."

- MICHAEL KORDA

29

"For me, singing sad songs is a way to heal a situation. It gets the hurt out in the open, into the light, out of the darkness."

- REBA MCENTIRE

30

"I was motivated to be different in part because I was different."

- DONNA BRAZILE

"I don't believe you have to be better than everybody else. I believe you have to be better than you ever thought you could be."

- KEN VENTURI

"A bird doesn't sing because it has an answer, it sings because it has a song."

- LOU HOLTZ

"I was forced to go to a positive-thinking seminar. I couldn't stand it. So I went outside to the parking lot and let half the air out of everybody's tires. As they came out I said, 'So …are your tires half full or half empty?"

- ADAM CHRISTING

"I think it's better to
dance than to march
through life."

– YOKO ONO

"One of the most
important lessons
I've learned is that
everyday things can be
fascinating. Instead of
trying to think up high-
concepts, I now look for
what's 'relatable'."

- JUDD APATOW

6

"PMS – the only time of month I can be myself."

- ROSEANNE BARR

7

"Truly wonderful the mind of a child is."

- YODA

"I remember a moment in my 30's when it suddenly dawned on me that if I went on delaying writing, I'd be a failed writer telling my grandchildren I'd desperately wanted to be a writer. I thought that would be appalling and I better make time and get started."

- P.D. James

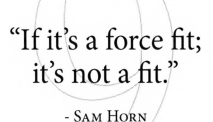

"If it's a force fit;
it's not a fit."

- SAM HORN

"Never hope
more than you work."

- RITA MAE BROWN

"If you want others to be happy, practice compassion. If you want to be happy, practice compassion."

- DALAI LAMA

"Words are small shapes in the gorgeous chaos of the world. They bring the world into focus, they corral ideas, they hone thoughts, they paint watercolors of perception."

- DIANE ACKERMAN

"A hero is someone who understands the responsibility that comes with his freedom."

- BOB DYLAN

When asked if he was always confident, Clint Eastwood said, "I don't think anybody starts out sure of himself. Otherwise it feels like arrogance. It's just that when you accept that life is a constant learning process, it becomes fun."

Asked why, at 72, he has no plans to retire, actor Morgan Freeman says, "If you take time off, you get more off than you want."

"I'm at an age where my back goes out more than I do."

- PHYLLIS DILLER

17

"It's just as easy to be nice as it is to be unpleasant, and the rewards are far greater."

- ALEX TREBEK

18

"When people anger you, they conquer you."

- TONI MORRISON

"My parents are my backbone. Still are. They're the only group that will support you if you score zero or you score 40."

- KOBE BRYANT

"The world changes when we change. The world softens when we soften. The world loves us when we choose to love the world."

- MARIANNE WILLIAMSON

21

"The heart of marriage
is memories."

- BILL COSBY

22

"If you don't like
something, change it.
If you can't change it,
change your attitude."

- MAYA ANGELOU

23

"Nothing ever goes away until it has taught us what we need to know."

- PEMA CHODRON

24

"Problems are messages."

- SHAKTI GAWAIN

"Music is forever; music should grow with you, following you right on up until you die."

— PAUL SIMON

"I think we're having fun. We're always trying to do better. We want to put a ding in the universe."

— STEVE JOBS

"If you worry about falling off the bike, you never get on."

- LANCE ARMSTRONG

"And the trouble is, if you don't ask anything, you risk even more."

- ERICA JONG

29

"Silence gives consent."

- OLIVER GOLDSMITH

30

"There must be more to life than having everything."

- MAURICE SENDAK

"The moment of victory
is much too short
to live for that
and nothing else."

- MARTINA NAVRATILOVA

"Technology is so much fun but we can drown in the fog of information which can drive out knowledge."

- DANIEL BOORSTIN

"I have seen many successful people fail after they start fearing they might lose what they have built."

- GUY LALIBERTE'

"A long marriage is two
people trying to dance
a duet and two solos
at the same time."

– ANNE TYLER

"The audience is the
best judge of anything.
They cannot be lied to.
Truth brings them closer.
A moment that lags -
they're gonna cough."

– BARBRA STREISAND

"Being a musician all started when I saw Kiss in the 70's. Watching them spit fire, I thought, 'Now, that's what I want to do.'"

- MATT NATHANSON

"What a lovely surprise to discover how unlonely being alone can be."

- ELLEN BURSTYN

7

"We'll hold out our hand; they have to unclench their fist."

- HILARY CLINTON

8

"We are what we pretend to be, so we better be careful what we pretend to be."

- KURT VONNEGUT

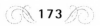

"When are you going
to realize that if it
doesn't apply to me,
it doesn't matter?"

- CANDACE BERGEN
IN TV SITCOM *MURPHY BROWN*

"Only in our dreams are
we free. The rest of the
time we need wages."

- TERRY PRATCHETT

"The world needs dreamers and the world needs doers. But above all, the world needs dreamers who do."

- SARAH BAN BREATHNACH

"Success without honor is an unseasoned dish; it will satisfy your hunger, but it won't taste good."

- COACH JOE PATERNO

13

"Humor does not
diminish the pain - it
makes the space around
it get bigger."

– Allen Klein

14

"I don't really cringe over
any of my albums."

– Sheryl Crow

"Before you build a better mousetrap, it helps to know if there are any mice out there."

- MORT ZUKERMAN

"I always wanted to be someone; I should have been more specific."

- LILLY TOMLIN

"Of one thing we can be sure. The quality of our life in the future will be determined by the quality of our thinking."

- EDWARD DE BONO

"I have ridiculously large dreams, and half the time they come true."

–DEBI THOMAS

19

"Intelligence is really
a kind of taste:
taste in ideas."

- SUSAN SONTAG

20

"Your intellect may
be confused, but your
emotions will never
lie to you."

- ROGER EBERT

"My mom says she learned how to swim when someone took her out in the lake and threw her off the boat. I said, 'Mom, they weren't trying to teach you how to swim."

– Paula Poundstone

"My girlfriend says I never listen to her. I think that's what she said."

- Drake Slather

23

"All the wrong people
have inferiority
complexes."

- COFFEE MUG SLOGAN

24

"The most valuable
possession you can
own is an open heart.
The most powerful
weapon you can be is an
instrument of peace."

— CARLOS SANTANA

"You've got to be original. If you're like everybody else; what do they need you for?"

— BERNADETTE PETERS

"Few people know so clearly what they want. Most people can't even think what to hope for when they throw a penny in a fountain."

— BARBARA KINGSOLVER

27

"A champion needs a motivation above and beyond winning."

- PAT RILEY

28

"Talking is all I ever wanted to do. When I was young it was called talking back; now it's called public speaking."

- FRAN LEBOWITZ

"When I work,
I work very hard.
So I look to work with
people who have that
level of dedication. And
I depend on that from
everyone. From
the director to my crews
that I work with."

– TOM CRUISE

"Imagination can carry
us to worlds that
never were."

- CARL SAGAN

"The person to negotiate with is the person who can deliver."

- RUDOLPH GIULIANI

"Let's give 'em something to talk about."

- BONNIE RAITT

"Trying to force
creativity
is never good."

- SARAH MCLAUGHLIN

"When you are
genuinely thrilled by
someone else's success,
it means you are on the
right track to your own."

– ESTHER HICKS

"I guess when you turn off the main road, you have to be prepared to see some funny houses."

-STEPHEN KING

"I am so busy doing nothing... that the idea of doing anything - which as you know, always leads to something - cuts into the nothing and then forces me to have to drop everything."

- JERRY SEINFELD

"We need to internalize this idea of excellence. Not many folks spend a lot of time trying to be excellent."

- BARACK OBAMA

"If the day is going bad and the prose isn't coming, I go into my library and look at my books and tell myself, 'I've done it before and I can do it again.'"

- DEAN KOONTZ

"Be nice to nerds.
Chances are you'll end
up working for one."

- BILL GATES

"Most people have no
idea of the giant capacity
we can immediately
command when
we focus all of our
resources on mastering a
single area of our lives."

– TONY ROBBINS

"Faith is the very first thing you should pack in a hope chest."

- SARAH BAN BREATHNACH

"I feel there are two people inside me - me and my intuition. If I go against her, she'll screw me every time, and if I follow her, we get along quite nicely."

- KIM BASINGER

"There are two kinds of people: the ones who need to be told and the ones who figure it out all by themselves."

— TOM CLANCY

"We are just an advanced breed of monkeys on a minor planet of a very average star. But we can understand the Universe. That makes us something very special."

- STEVEN W. HAWKING

15

"If you don't know where you're going, you'll end up somewhere else."

- Yogi Berra

16

"My wife made me get these glasses. I wasn't seeing things her way."

- Mark Klein

17

"Great minds like a think."

– SLOGAN OF THE ECONOMIST

18

"Once you've done the mental work, there comes a point you have to throw yourself into action and put your heart on the line."

- PHIL JACKSON

"I don't look to jump over 7-foot bars: I look around for 1-foot bars that I can step over."

- WARREN BUFFETT

"Time is free, but it's priceless. You can't own it, but you can use it. You can't keep it, but you can spend it. Once you've lost it you can never get it back."

- HARVEY MACKAY

"Music is healing. It's an explosive expression of humanity. No matter what culture we're from, it's something we are all touched by."

- BILLY JOEL

"When an idea reaches critical mass there is no stopping the shift its presence will induce."

- MARIANNE WILLIAMSON

"Things can fall apart,
or threaten to, for many
reasons, and then there's
got to be a leap of faith.
Ultimately, when you're
at the edge, you have to
go forward or backward;
if you go forward, you
have to jump together."

- YO-YO MA

"The grass looks greener on the other side, but it still needs to be mowed."

- JOEL OSTEEN

"You don't get into committed relationships with jokes – you become kind of promiscuous in that you're always looking to see what other jokes are out there."

- SETH MEYERS

"I'm always looking for something to engage my imagination and take me on a little voyage. I just want a new topic in my life."

- STEVE MARTIN

"I intend to live forever. So far, so good."

- STEVEN WRIGHT

"What is guilt? Guilt is the pledge drive constantly hammering in our heads that keeps us from fully enjoying the show…"

- DENNIS MILLER

"I've left just about every vacation I've ever had. After 3 days, I'm bored. I'd just as soon go somewhere and tell a story."

- ANDERSON COOPER

"It's rare to find a consistently insightful person who is also an angry person. They can't occupy the same space. If your anger moves in, generosity and creativity move out."

– SETH GODIN

"Our concern must be to live while we're alive... To release our inner selves from the spiritual death that comes with living behind a facade designed to conform to external definitions of who and what we are."

- ELIZABETH KUBLER-ROSS

How to Use Quotes for MIV –
Maximum Intrigue Value

"No one wants to go out in mid-sentence."

ACTOR JOHNNY DEPP

Why is it important – and advantageous - to focus on and feature new quotes?

My dad was the one who taught me that introducing "haven't heard that before" insights is a way to be one-of-a-kind instead of one-of-many.

I was selected to be valedictorian for my eighth-grade graduation.

I know. You may be thinking, "Big whoop," but this was a small town (35 kids in our graduating class) and I was all of 12 years old . . . so this was a big deal for me.

A week before the big day, I asked my father to critique my eight-minute talk.

Dad, Warren Reed, was Director of Vocational Agriculture Education for the State of California and oversaw the Future Farmers of America program. FFA is committed to developing speaking skills in young people because it believes the ability to speak clearly, confidently, and convincingly is as important to professional success as talent, education and hard work.

Dad had judged many speaking competitions on the state and national levels, and was a respected public speaker who learned how to be comfortable in front of a group from his father, George Reed who was the president of Toastmasters International in 1951.

Dad patiently listened to my "bird ready to leave the nest and fly on its own" homily that was the central theme of my talk.

When I finished, he was silent for a moment, then said simply, "It's a good enough talk, but you didn't say anything that hasn't already been said in a thousand other commencement speeches."

Dad wasn't being mean; he knew I wanted honest feedback and was just doing what he could to help me be a better speaker.

He continued, "Sam, if you're going to ask people for their valuable time and attention, it is your responsibility to say something original."

"But Dad, there's nothing new under the sun."

He smiled and said, "Sure there is. Want to know what the definition of 'original' is? If we haven't heard it before, it's original."

That started my life-long quest to create original content and share fresh quotes people haven't heard before. . . . so they don't nod off mid-sentence.

People are delighted when we introduce pithy, profound observations that make them reflect, smile and reconsider what they thought they knew to be true.

At this point, you may be saying, "Sam, you're preaching to the choir. I already believe in the power of quotes; that's why I bought this book. What I want to know is, 'How can I integrate them into my written and spoken material to maximize their value?'"

Here's how.

How to Use Quotes to Get Eyebrows Up – Smart-phones Down

> "As Spinoza, or someone very much like him, once said . . ."
> AUTHOR JUDITH VIORST

There's an art and a craft to integrating quotations on the page, stage, online and in person so they pass the Eyebrow Test® and (hopefully) have a long tail of influence.

Here are just a few of the tips I share with my consulting clients and audiences on how to seamlessly and strategically incorporate quotes into your work to spice it up and add enduring value for all involved.

Quote Usage Tip # 1
Steer Clear of Common Quotes

"When I go to movies, one of my strongest desires
is to be shown something new. I want to go to new
places, meet new people, have new experiences.
When I see Hollywood formulas mindlessly
repeated, a little something dies inside of me. I have
lost two hours to boors who insist on telling me
stories I've heard before."

– FILM CRITIC ROGER EBERT

Roger is right. We all yearn to be shown something new. As soon as someone trots out a ubiquitous quote or makes an obvious statement, a little something inside us dies.

If you've heard it before, your audience has heard it before. They sigh and tune out because their first impression is you're not worth listening to because you're not saying anything new.

For example, Marianne Williamson has a powerful quote about "playing small" (often misattributed to Nelson Mandela) that says:

"Our deepest fear is not that
we are inadequate.
Our deepest fear is that we are
powerful beyond measure.
It is our light, not our darkness
that most frightens us.
We ask ourselves, 'Who am I to be brilliant,
gorgeous, talented, fabulous?'
Actually, who are you not to be? Your playing small
does not serve the world.
There is nothing enlightened about shrinking
so other people won't feel insecure around you.
We are all meant to shine, as children do.
As we let our own light shine, we unconsciously give other
people permission to do the same."

That's a thought-provoking quote; however, it's also a very popular quote.

Chances are, you've heard it in presentations or read it online. You may even have it tacked up on your wall or posted on your refrigerator. If you found this book on a shelf and skimmed through the pages to see if it's worth buying - and you saw that quote and several others like it that are already in your mental library – you'd put the book back. Why buy a book that's full of things you already know?

On the other hand, if you skimmed through a book and everything you saw was new to you, you'd conclude, "This will be worth my time, mind, and dime."

A colleague once asked me about her favorite quote from Eleanor Roosevelt. She is a former beauty pageant winner who speaks on self-esteem to high school students. She said, "Sam, I know these girls have no idea who Eleanor Roosevelt is, but I love her insight that 'No one can make you feel inferior without your consent.' It makes my point perfectly and I can't bear to leave it out. What should I do?"

I told her, "If that's the case – if a quote truly is perfect for your purposes or particularly meaningful to you; then anticipate your audience's negative reaction and neutralize it with a disclaimer such as, "I imagine some of you are thinking, 'Who the heck is Eleanor Roosevelt?' Well, she was a powerful first lady – much like Michelle Obama – and I promise to quote Beyonce' and other people you know from here on out . . . "

If you let people know why you're including a familiar quote or an unfamiliar source - why you feel this saying is worth repeating because it's significant to you, this topic or their circumstances – they'll buy in.

Quote Usage Tip # 2
Mix It Up

"Your opening has to be good – or the rest of the story
won't have a chance because nobody
will stick around to read it."

– AUTHOR LAWRENCE BLOCK

If you want to appeal to a diverse audience, be sure to feature a kaleidoscope of quotes in the first few moments (or pages) and keep a gender, ethnic, age, geographical and industry balance in your sources.

Any extreme will quickly become noticeable and potentially

offensive. If you quote only men, only Caucasians, only athletes, only Americans, that could become a turnoff. People won't stick around because they'll conclude you're not talking to "them."

Quote Usage Tip # 3
Feature A Variety Of Classic and Contemporary Sources, Relevant To Your Audience

The best of all worlds is to tap into the wisdom of our elders and of modern-day icons so our communication is both timeless and timely. By quoting everyone from Plato to Paul Simon, you add unpredictability to your work which is always good because people don't know what's coming next. It keeps them on their mental toes.

Yes, I've featured only current quotes in this book –but that's because most quotes sites/sources out there focus primarily on quotes from thought-leaders who lived hundreds of years ago. Who the heck is Pliny the Elder??

I'll always remember the day I was speaking to a group of college students about changing their approach from "I'm just looking for a job" to "I'm creating my dream career." To address their skepticism, I quoted Robert H. Goddard, "It is difficult to say what is impossible, for the dream of yesterday is the hope of today and the reality of tomorrow."

The problem? I neglected to tell the group who Goddard was. They looked at me, puzzled, and were ready to write me off until I put things in context by explaining he was a "rocket scientist," (NASA's Goddard Space Center is named after him), and he's credited with being a founding father of space flight. I then "hooked & hinged" Goddard's quote to how these grads could give flight to their dreams.

And then there was the time I quoted Jane Fonda while conducting a Public Speaking workshop for the U.S. Navy . . . Not a good idea. At the time, Jane was famous (infamous?) for protesting the Vietnam War, and these military officers did not appreciate the fact that I was using her as an example.

Learn from my mistakes. Do your homework so anyone you hold up as an example meets your customers' approval. If you're speaking internationally or writing a blog that's distributed around the world, be sure to quote current thought-leaders from different countries so you truly are going global.

Quote Usage Tip # 4
Be Funny and Philosophical –
Emotional and Logical

"Life abounds in humor
if you just look around."

– MEL BROOKS

Make 'em laugh; make 'em think.

Adding humor causes people to like you; adding insights causes people to learn from you.

Featuring laugh-out-loud quotes alongside introspective quotes gives people an emotional roller-coaster experience. It's a way to appeal to left and right brainers and be the steak and the sizzle.

You can add gravitas and substance to your remarks by quoting startling statistics or recent research from *Wall Street Journal* or *Investor's Business Daily*. You can add wit and wisdom to your remarks by quoting world-class athletes, celebrities or comedians.

A favorite is Judy Tenuta who said, "My parents always told me I wouldn't amount to anything because I procrastinated so much. I told 'em, 'Just you wait.'"

If you're a tax attorney, you could then segue into your point by asking, "Are you waiting until April 14th to do your taxes?" If you're a personal trainer, you could dovetail into, "Are you waiting until you have more time to get back to the gym? Do you know anyone who has more time now than they did last year?"

Remember, if it makes you laugh, chances are it will make others laugh. Follow Mel Brooks' advice and keep your antenna up for the humor that is all around. When something gets a chuckle from you, write it down and figure out how to incorporate it into an upcoming communication.

Quote Usage Tip # 5
Always Attribute

"As a reader, I want a book
to kidnap me into its world."
- AUTHOR ERICA JONG

It's okay to quote other people's insights; it's not okay to kidnap other people's insights. In fact, it's unethical and illegal to repeat other people's wisdom verbatim and try to pass it off as your own.

Just like a piano player riffs off standard chords to improvise and create new music; the goal is to riff off (not rip off) standard quotes and extrapolate their essence to create new aha's.

In today's online, all-the-time digital world; it's not enough to simply "give credit where credit is due." When possible, include a link to that person's website or blog, refer to their book or business, or direct people to their Twitter, Facebook page or You Tube channel so you're honoring originators.

You have an opportunity to spread their work and make that person go viral which is a way of creating a rising tide of wisdom that raises everyone's boat.

Quote Usage Tip # 6
Deliver Quotes Without Notes

> "At first it's a bit jagged, awkward, but then
> there's a point where there's a click and
> you suddenly become quite fluent."
>
> – AUTHOR DORIS LESSING

Quick. When and where was the last conference or business meeting you attended?

What can you remember of what was said? What can you repeat, word for word, of what you heard?

If you can't repeat anything, the communication from that meeting is "out of sight, out of mind." All the money, time and effort spent in getting to that event pretty much went down the tubes. All the time, money and effort those speakers/meeting planners spent trying to favorably impact you was for naught.

If you want enduring impact, you've got to take responsibility for saying something so profound, people can't wait to repeat it to others.

If you want 25 innovative ways to make your material intriguing and enduring so it POP!s, you can find them in my book *POP! Create the Perfect Pitch, Title and Tagline for Anything* which has been sold around the world (U.S.,

China, Europe, South America) and featured in the *New York Times, Washington Post,* FastCompany.com, MSNBC and BusinessWeek.com.

If you want to know how to deliver a quote so it captures the attention of busy, distracted people, get a copy of *The Eyebrow Test®, Intrigue Anyone in Anything in 60 Seconds.*

Here are just a few of the recommendations excerpted from those books on how to increase a quote's MIV – Maximum Intrigue Value.

You want a quote to stand out – and for IT to stand out – YOU'VE got to stand out.

Reading a quote from a teleprompter, script or your notes is a prescription for blending in. And blending in is for Cuisinarts – not for communicators.

One of the most meaningful compliments ever given me was by Arthur Levine from Scholastic. Arthur brought the Harry Potter series to the United States and was a keynoter at the Maui Writers Conference (which I emceed for 17 years). He came up to me after the first day and said, "Sam, I love the way you talk – you put space around your words." That from J. K. Rowling's editor. Made my day!

Your goal is to go from being awkward and jagged – to being fluent and impactful – and one way to do that is to put space around an important quote by pausing before it…and after it.

You wouldn't race through a fine dinner, don't race through a fine quote.

If you rush your words, they'll go in one ear, out the other. Slow down. Savor this profound insight. Say it slowly and e-l-o-n-g-a-t-e the words so you're verbally caressing them. That way, you give people an opportunity to mull over this profound quote and absorb it, appreciate it, adopt it. That gives your powerful insight its MIV – Maximum Intrigue Value.

Are you thinking: "What if the quote I want to use is too long to memorize?"

Hmmm… that quote may be too long to use. Remember, if they can't repeat it, they didn't get it.

You may want to excerpt that quote into its quintessence. There is often a pearl of wisdom in a long quote that is more powerful on its own than when buried in several sentences.

And if you're writing a book, blog, article or column? Give an important quote its own line.

That way, it's a lot more likely to POP! out of the text and get noticed and remembered . . .for all the right reasons.

It's Okay, Even Advisable, To Quote Yourself

"Everyone is entitled to my opinion."

- MADONNA

I used to think it was egotistical to quote yourself. I now understand that if you create a new word (NURD) or one-of-a-kind phrase and don't credit yourself, you've just sold yourself short and forfeited all the "google juice," career visibility and money you deserve to make from your creativity.

I learned this the hard way. Over my twenty-five years as a keynote speaker/author, I've done my best to follow my father's advice about being "original," so I've been diligent about creating my own intellectual capital.

In my books *Tongue Fu!*®, *POP!*, *Take the Bully by the Horns*, *What's Holding You Back*, *ConZentrate*, and the upcoming *SerenDestiny*, I've coined first-of-their-kind titles and terminology and have crafted many a proprietary "phrase that pays." But, for years, I didn't officially put my name on these phrases or attempt to copyright or trademark them. As a result, other people ran with them and turned them into profitable domains, book titles, presentations and products.

As my sons would say, "My bad."

So you may notice that I quote myself several times in this book. That's not conceit or ego. I've done that on purpose to model that if you create a money phrase, you need to credit yourself for it. In these days of multi-million dollar domain names and brand names, you deserve to profit from your intellectual capital. It's naïve to think or do otherwise.

How Can I Find More Current Quotes?

"If you stick to what you know;
you sell yourself short."

- CARRIE UNDERWOOD

I agree with Carrie Underwood. I firmly believe almost any communication can be improved with a current, relevant quote from a respected source that sheds new light on a topic.

One way to tap into the day's "zeitgeist" is to keep your antenna up when reading newspapers and magazines, watching the news, movies and your favorite TV shows.

My consulting clients know the value of "props." Holding up that morning's newspaper and referencing something that was in the headlines lets their audience know this isn't a rehearsed-to-death spiel. One client held up the sponsoring association's industry magazine and quoted a line from the incoming chair's mission statement. Suffice it to say, she was a big hit because she was one of the only speakers to do her homework and demonstrate she cared by integrating a quote from one of the hosts.

If you are a trainer or manager who is leading an orientation, conducting a team-building session or heading up a customer service workshop; featuring a recent quote that refers to a frustration everyone shares is a way of creating a community because people feel they're "in on the joke."

For example, Sandra Bernhard was on one of the late-night talk shows. The host was saying how rude it is for people to check their cell phones while sharing dinner. He said he had caller ID and never answered the phone in public unless it was crucial. The quick-witted Bernhard said, "Yah, caller ID helps, but what I'm waiting for is . . . caller IQ."

Introducing a witty zinger like that – instead of just trotting out how-to's - can make you seem hip instead of ho-hum. If you write or speak about etiquette and modern day manners; you could reference that line and then hook and hinge it into, "Until we have Caller IQ . . . here are 5 cell-phone tips you can use to communicate more graciously in business situations."

Scanning *USA Today* or the *Wall St. Journal* the morning of a presentation, whether it's to your board of directors or a weekly staff meeting, is one of the best five-minute investments you can make.

When you find something that pertains to your issue, cut it out (or print it out if it's online) and bring it with you so you can share the pertinent statistic, quote, or paragraph with your group. And yes, you can read it off your digital device if you prefer. The fact that you went above and beyond to do something unexpected will pleasantly surprise your audience and further raise your approval ratings.

For example, if you're a basketball fan, you may be familiar with the feud that existed between former L.A. Laker teammates seven-foot tall Shaquille O'Neil and Kobe Bryant. Insults were exchanged in person and in the press, and the two notoriously avoided even looking at each other in 2005 when they faced each other on the court.

Their very public spat came to an end on Martin Luther King Day in 2006. O'Neil, then playing for the Miami Heat, approached Bryant during the pre-game warm-ups and extended the olive branch. After a short conversation, the longtime adversaries shook hands and shared a hug at center court.

What inspired O'Neil to do this? "I had orders from the great Hall of Famer Bill Russell," O'Neil said. "Martin Luther King was an ambassador of peace. Bill Russell told me I should honor his birthday today and shake Kobe Bryant's hand and let bygones be bygones and bury the hatchet."

In my mind, O'Neil demonstrated what a "big man" he truly is by initiating that peacemaking gesture. If you're a consultant working with a group that's mired in conflict; instead of being content to share platitudes about how important it is to get along, you could hold up that article, read O'Neil's words, and let his shining example eloquently make your point for you about letting go of grudges.

Quoting a respected individual who has successfully done what you're recommending lets that individual do your talking for you. It's a way of saying, "You don't have to take my word on this. Here's proof this is valid and it works." It's a Socratic face-saving way for people to choose to change – not because they're being told to - but because they want to.

How to Hook and Hinge Quotes so They're Relevant for Everyone

"Remember, you're more interested in what you have to say than anyone else is."

–ANDY ROONEY, 60 MINUTES

What does "hook and hinge" mean? Well, let me demonstrate what happens when a communicator doesn't do this – and then we'll explain what it is and show how to do it. Sound good?

I'll always remember an Olympic medal-winner who delivered the opening keynote for a conference I was attending. He went into great detail about the trials and tribulations on his way to becoming a world-class athlete. He told us how excited he was to earn a place on the Olympic team, and his misery after choking at the Games and not even finishing in the top ten.

His resulting depression caused him to quit his sport. He then moved into the "uplifting" part of his presentation in which he realized he loved competing and wouldn't be happy unless he gave it one more try. He wrapped up with a play-by-play description of his winning performance and trip to the medal stand.

The audience gave him a polite standing ovation; however, as I looked around the room, I could tell many were thinking, "Well, good for you. But how's that help me?"

Never once in his presentation did he "hook and hinge" his message back to the audience and ask how his lessons-learned might be relevant or useful for them.

Never once did he ask, "Did you ever set a goal and work hard for it? Did things not turn out the way you hoped? Were you tempted to throw in the towel? Did you? Later, did you realize you'd never forgive yourself if you didn't give it one more try? Did you persevere through the ups-and-downs and accomplish what you set out do to? Do you remember that sweet feeling of 'I did it!'"

His presentation wasn't about the audience and *their* goals. It was all about him. Me, me, me.

He could have turned that one-way monologue into a two-way dialogue if he'd followed each major insight (or quote) in his presentation with three "hook and hinge YOU questions" that switched the focus to his audience and gave them an opportunity to relate this point to their circumstances.

Why do I call these "hook and hinge You Questions"? That's easy. They contain the word "you" in them and they make your communication about your readers, viewers, listeners instead of it being an exercise in narcissism. Posing at least 3 questions with the word "you" in them increases the likelihood everyone will have experienced – or is experiencing - something in their personal or professional life that's similar to what you just said.

Now *your* story – or insight or lesson-learned - has become their story, insight or lesson-learned.

"You questions" shake people out of their reverie. They engage everyone's mind's eye and imagination and transform a data dump or lecture into an interaction where you are hooking your content and hinging it to their circumstances.

How do you come up with those "You Questions"? First you identify the "hook" of the quote you just shared. What's the key word or phrase? What's the main point , primary word or key take-way?

Now, visualize your target customers/readers/listeners/viewers/decision-makers . . and get in their head. Ask yourself what you could ask that would give everyone reading this, listening to this or seeing this an opportunity to relate it to their circumstances.

For example, if you quoted Mitch Albom's "I am in love with hope", the words "hope" and "love" are the hooks. Now, hinge back to your audience with three questions that cause them to think about the role – for better or for worse – *hope* plays in their life. For example:

- What are you in love with?
- Are you in love with hope – or with fear?
- How can you fill yourself with hope instead of fear – and focus on what you DO want vs. what you DON'T want?

Your goal is to select three diverse questions so everyone hearing them will instantly relate to at least one.

It's worth emphasizing this again because it's so crucial.

Investing time into selecting and crafting "You questions" to tie your quotes back to your topic and audience can be a communication deal-maker or deal-breaker. They turn a "So what's that got to do with me?" reaction into an "I see how this relates to me" response.

When done well, these "hooks" (the key phrase, punch-line or resonant words of your quote) are "hinged" into your content so seamlessly, people are more likely to relate to them, remember them, repeat them, recommend them and act on them in the days, weeks and months ahead.

And be sure to "call back" to your most powerful quotes at the end of your presentation or copy. If you don't reference it one last time at the end of your text or speech, it will be out of sight, out of mind.

As a communicator, you want to keep your message top of mind. If you do a good job of introducing pithy, profound insights and hooking and hinging them to your group, people will become your word-of-mouth advertisers and take you and them viral.

And isn't that what we want? To share powerful, positive communication that favorably impacts people who pass it on so our messages scale and reach even more people? If you use these tips for integrating current quotes into your communication, you'll be the one they remember and you'll be the one they'll want to read, watch, listen to and engage with . . . again and again.

We Want to Hear From You

At The Intrigue Institute, we're always looking for new current quotes that will engage people's imagination and introduce a fresh approach for our conversations and written and spoken communication.

Want to help?

Keep your antenna up for intriguing individuals, events and organizations. When you hear or see a quote from a current celebrity, athlete or thought-leader that "has you at hello," take a moment to send it to us at info@SamHorn.com and put "Intriguing Quote" in the subject heading.

With your permission, we'll include it in a blog post, newsletter, corporate or convention presentation or on our website.

We'll be glad to make this a win-win by crediting you, mentioning your website, blog or social media site and sending you our Top 10 Favorite Current Quotes (which are constantly being updated.)

Want more information about Sam Horn and the Intrigue Institute? Interested in Sam's products, consulting services and programs about how to intrigue anyone in anything in 60 seconds? Visit www.SamHorn.com and www.IntrigueInstitute. com and www.SamHornPOP.wordpress.com.

If you're planning a convention or program, you can hire Sam or one of our Intrigue Institute speakers to share their inspiring message that will have your audience on the edge of their seats.

Our client list includes Cisco, Intel, NASA, Hewlett-Pack-ard, Boeing, SCORE, Boeing, KPMG, Genentech, ASAE, National Governors Association, the annual Inc. 500/5000 conference, Entrepreneurs Organization and many international audiences.

You're welcome to contact us at 1 800 SAM-3455 and tell us about your program and we'll gladly discuss Sam's availability and fees and discuss how she can customize a program for your group.

Sam Horn, the founder of the Intrigue Institute and creator of this *Current Quotes* book, has been featured on MSNBC, NPR, Jay Leno's Tonight Show, on BusinessWeek.com and FastCompany.com and in the *Washington Post, Investor's Business Daily, Boston Globe* and the *New York Times*.

If you would like to interview Sam for your TV or radio show or if you'd like to write a profile of the Intrigue Institute's mission to showcase interesting insights from today's top icons, influencers and innovators – contact her at Sam@SamHorn. com and put MEDIA INTERVIEW in the subject heading.

If you'd like to receive a weekly Current Quote-a-Gram that comes with a beautiful image (and NO selling), subscribe by emailing Sam@SamHorn.com and putting CURRENT QUOTE-A-GRAM in the subject heading.

And, if you'd like to connect with Sam via social media – connect with her at the following:

Twitter: @SamHorn_dot_com

Face Book: Sign-on to your account and seach "Sam Horn"

Find out when Sam will be speaking in your area – and what new quotes she discovered that day.

We look forward to hearing from you.

Index by Author

Index by Topic

DID YOU LIKE THESE CURRENT
QUOTES? WANT MORE?
OKAY – YOU ASKED FOR IT.
HERE THEY ARE!

**Visit: www.SamHorn.com
To purchase our newest books:**

*MORE Current Quotes:
Intriguing Insights from Today's
Top Athletes, Actors, Inventors,
Executives and Ideapreneurs*

*Current Quotes for Creative Souls:
Intriguing Insights from Today's
Top Authors and Artists*

*Almost Current Quotes:
Intriguing Insights from 1990 - 2010*

HERE ARE SAMPLES FROM OUR OTHER BOOKS:

"A hero is someone who understands the responsibility that comes with his freedom."
– BOB DYLAN

"I don't use the word perfect because nothing's ever perfect. I strive for *excellence*."
– BARBRA STREISAND

"I want compassion to be the new black."
– STEPHEN TYLER

"A day without sunshine is like, you know, night."
– STEVE MARTIN

"All you umpires, back to the bleachers. Referees, hit the showers. It's my game. I pitch, hit, catch, run the bases. At sunset, I've won or lost. At sunrise, I'm out again, giving it the old try."
– RAY BRADBURY

"Success is not about getting it done or attaining money and stuff. The measure of success in life is absolutely the amount of joy you feel."
– ESTHER HICKS

"My new motto is, 'When you're through changing,
you're through.'"
– MARTHA STEWART

"Science is a way of thinking more than it is a body
of knowledge."
– CARL SAGAN

"Life happens at the level of events, not of words.
Trust movement."
– ALFRED ADLER

"In life as in dance: grace glides on blistered feet."
– ALICE ABRAMS

"My creativity comes in spurts."
– BARBRA STREISAND

"Oh, you hate your job? Why didn't you say so?
There's a support group for that.
It's called *everybody*."
– DREW CARY

"It's rare to find a consistently creative or insightful
person who is also an angry person. They can't
occupy the same space, and if your anger moves in,
generosity and creativity often move out."
– SETH GODIN

"I always try to dance when this song comes on because I am the queen and I like to dance."
– QUEEN ELIZABETH II,
TO STARTLED ONLOOKERS WHEN SHE STARTED DANCING TO ABBA's "DANCING QUEEN" AT A DINNER PARTY

"My mother never thought I could become anything. I am grateful to her for that because it made me who I am."
– BARBRA STREISAND

When asked if she worries about losing her voice, Barbara Streisand said, "No. I never vocalize around the house or do scales in the shower. When I love the music I'm singing, it's just *there* for me."
THESE QUOTES ARE FROM AUG. 21, 2011
CBS SUNDAY MORNING INTERVIEW

"Time is an equal-opportunity employer. Each human being has exactly the same number of hours every day. Rich people can't buy more hours. Scientists can't invent new minutes. You can't save time to spend it on another day. Even so, time is amazingly fair and forgiving. No matter how much time you've wasted in the past, you still have an entire tomorrow."
– DENIS WAITLEY

"My mom says she learned how to swim when someone took her out in the lake and threw her off the boat. I said, 'Mom, they weren't trying to teach you how to swim.'"

– Paula Poundstone

Women are the most powerful magnet in the universe. All men are cheap metal and we know where North is."

– Larry Miller

"When you are genuinely thrilled by someone else's success, that means you are right on the track of your own."

– Esther Hicks

"I wish my mouth had a backspace key."

– A Popular Tweet

"Two monologues do not make a dialogue."

– Jeff Daly

CPSIA information can be obtained at www.ICGtesting.com
Printed in the USA
BVOW040436011211

277175BV00001B/6/P